About the Weather
Spring Trending

Marie Lynam Fitzptrick

About the Weather

Spring Trending

Published by The Linnet's Wings, 2015
ISBN-13: 978-0993049330

Visit www.thelinnetswings.org to read more about our publication.

Also by The Linnet's Wings:

The Song of Hiawatha by Henry Wadsworth Longfellow:
ISBN-13: 978-1480176423
One Day Tells its Tale to Another by Nonnie Augustine:
ISBN-13: 978-1480186354
Randolph Caldecott's The House that Jack Built: ISBN-13:
978-1483977669
About the Weather. Spring Trending by Marie Lynam
Fitzpatrick:ISBN-13: 978-0993049330
This Crazy Urge to Live by Bobby Steve Baker: ISBN: 978-
0993049-0-9

Acknowledgments

We are lifted into postions by others that we meet along our way. My small poetry contribution would not have made it into the market place without the support and help that I have received from the writers over in the "Zoetrope Virtual Studio," and the team at "The Linnet's Wings" literary magazine. It's a big thank you to the guys.

I want also to thank Peter Gilkes for his constant support. I work with Peter on a day to day basis and his attention to detail and his focus never ceases to astound me.

Marie Fitzpatrick

Dedication

For my mum, my family, my children and my grandchildren

CONTENTS

Epigraph

When wishes are dashed from butterfly wings
We dream to wake and wake to dream

MLF 2009

xv

JANUARY

December homage has been made.
Dark drifts but light slips into days
Where caterpillars await chrysalis,
And west winds clean the sky,
And waves splash froth,
As a year gets set for new beginnings.

TREEHOUSE SHIPS

It's a blowsy rain that stirs the wind.
To annoy the trees it shakes their leaves,
It bends their boughs

This ebb and flow a tidal surge
That lifts the nests—disturbs the birds.
But holding fast these weathered mates

Adrift in storm just batten down.
So that when cloud sweeps in and day is dark
And they're locked down I miss life's stars.

SWEEP

Each day the waves are rolling lines of sea
Green sweep that lifts to drop then flounce,
Before making frilly, frothy, lacy threads

That wind works through to make beach sounds.
Unchanged since time began, her script is set in
Graceful dance that's timed by moons in cloistered nights,

Assuring one in chequered day that play
And grace and love and hope is all around:
That they've been marking time since time began.

THE GERUND

Here wind and clouds are sharing blow
With chimes that ping and push;
And rush about collecting glow
To feed spring's growth—her early blush

That's settling in now winter's gone.
Last week I saw an S appear
In clouds that imaged swans.
Today P showed in brownish tear

That opened in a layered sky
And towed a R, and then went back
To fetch the S from way up high.
This SPR's now framed on skys' new plaque;

And the land awaits the glow of sun.
An ING is all she needs, a gerund,
To swing the clock's old pun,
To waken folk to spring day fun.

DOWNSIDEUPSIDEDOWN

Today when sun lit in day
She turned our world around.
Instead of climbing in the same old way
To drop her vision down,

She rode into a dancing bay,
And drowned the west in rainbow sounds.
It took a while for folk to see
The new life that day had found,

And they went to shop, to school, to work,
And all were full of glee.
Then when sundown came those in town
Looked west, yes! they looked west to see

Day's colour set in waves—unbound,
But! sun fell east into the sea.
And known scores were run around,
And worlds turned downsideupsidedown.

SPRING SPINS OUT

The sky's a chequerboard of grey and white,
And temps. are up and folk are out.
It's calm, it's Lent, and time is ticking—quiet.
Look-up! lead clouds are dressed—all-out.

The count is on as spring spins out in haze.
Ripped beats are shifting towards her mystery;
Lustrous filing of drama's tales from olden days,
Repetitive as this seasons' history.

ON LOUGH BOFIN

From pressing clouds snow fell today.
Large white drops clutched the air to float and spin.
And in the harbour pen slept—her image stayed,
Statued in ice, her head hid in her wing.

Along the harbour path a boy and girl ran,
And air lit-up as a memory was writ.
Later it will be used to make happy plans,
And they'll stretch and ease into a graceful drift.

WEBS

Well the sun broke through: The sky is blue.
Her colour shades from babe to air force tints,
And now that day is clear folk can view
The beauty that she hid within the hints.

This wind that blew the webs away
Set out to shade the light with dark,
But she floundered in a sparkling bay
Where beauty just rubbed out her mark.

IN PRAISE OF RAIN

Splash splosh hopping drops
Beat against the window panes.
Raining sheets, beating down,
Causing all about to frown.

Umbrellas everywhere,
Matching shoes and outerware.
O there's stylish folk about,
It just took the rain to bring them out!

FEBRUARY

Old bones are soaking up the light.
Seeds are shooting up; winds puff
Up scents and flowers are opening
To suit the weather. As her light
Deflects the dark February suits herself:
She introduces the business of living well.

And here, in Andalusia, day sits easy
For life is loved-up. A charm has been born
Under dawns' spills and wrapped in
Dusks' embrace, and as fig branches sprout,
Colour rinses out a beauty that will
Be lusciously garnished later in summer.

But just for now Eros takes time to plant,
So that lovers and love can bless time.

AGAINST THE WIND

Today the west wind sweeps the sky,
She's out, she's strong: In fighting form,
She adds light twinkle to February sighs,
And people are drawn in by this old storm
That flirts with sun, and the Med's awash with joy.
Her feisty light gives treats in spray that pounds
And sprinkles life through barmy ploys:
But it's impish, jesting, brave and sound.

But who knows where this wind will fall?
It's east she buffets as she glowers,
For as she leans against her trades they crawl,
Then stop to start again collecting power.

This love that runs against the wind,
Just knows that wind inspires kin.

Marie Lynam Fitzpatrick

THE SPRING MARCH

Today's bearing was clear.
The sun shone from early morning.
But cold winds rumble in the air:
It's a damp forewarning.

And people are polite.
Goods are well priced.
Banks advertise a cashless sobriety;
This Irish Water March has been well sliced and iced.

Swinging hot to cold, sun to snow,
Teasing with promises of a warm spring—
An uncommon luxury—a dice throw.
For who really knows what she'll bring?

Judiciary has ruled against their own.
And fat clouds weight down with rain.
Who knows what seeds have been sown!
Who will make ground from this gain?

COMPOSITION

Last night a sea swept low then high.
It stirred the air with crashing waves,
And wind picked up her moaning cry,
And set her notes onto a stave.

They climbed up and down and on and off,
To hum, to strum, and bum sympathy.
And in the sky the clouds played
Out their tune—they stopped and stared

And beamed and flit—they bayed
Back down but were back lit by care.
By stars that twinkled happy days,
Just out of sight behind a door

Where a sandy beach laid–
Out love tunes remembered from one's time before.
When skies were clear and sun made art,
And from a golden chain fell a claddagh heart.

SUNSET AT LA CHUCHA

The sky is electrified tonight.
The wind has stirred a rainbow up.
She's sat in cloud hemming tears
With deepened red and purple threads
That she's layered over velvet grey.
She's puffed them up and spun them out.

And lacy greens and pinks shine through
Wind's blow—that echoes through her glow,
And tangles with the squalling sea,
Who calls to sun to fall to leave,
To rise above another day,
As storm draws in and night falls down.

THE LIFT

The morning drives a windy, rainy grey
That's settled over fields and lakes.
From dawn the rain fell hard to splash and splay,
And with no let-up it runs down streets and shakes

Through trees—a wild cadence
That gambles with life's Lenten stakes.
And as she cuts her teeth on poetic aidance
An ancient story shows the way:

It was the first to make the break,
To anchor man in a just day.
Now one attends the Easter wake
To watch life skit in shades of grey.

FEBRUARY PUTS ON A DRESS

The sun is dancing on the sea
     She is dressed in blue and white
        And her hair trails
            Through a solf breeze
                That twinkles with all the colour
                    That is trapped within the world
                In a snow globe that rolls and rolls
            Across the waves of peace
        And frustrates the wind
    That shouts and screams
            Against the soft force of the season
                Today, in Andalucía, February is lilting

GIRL ASLEEP UNDER STARS

I found the Sun outside today,
Her air spread out on scent.
Spring's summer preview was an exposé,
That hoovered just a while then went.
Sun sleeps like a girl asleep under stars
That shadow her face like prison bars.
She waits on a sign from the harebell.
To colour the heavenly airs.
For its perfume plays-out a springtime knell
That accompanies sweet springs' prayer.
And Sun is the girl asleep under stars
That shadow her face like prison bars.

PERFORMANCE

This morning found Febuary cold still here.
There was a mourning feel about the play.
Her light was blind, there was no sparkling air,
As actors made their way about the day.

Then suddenly the sun came in to sing.
And light and life jumped on a roundabout,
That whizzed so fast the players jumped to bring
An offering to this grace that she churned-out.

And ease set in as day went on to trade
The cold for scented jasmine flavoured flair,
And peace was found in gentle windless shade,
And purring doves made love—a speechless prayer.

SUNDAY READY, LAKEPOINT

Has thrilling blackbirds framed in green,
And thrushes fluffing up their breasts.

And angels squiggling an inky sheen,
In skies dressed for Sunday guests.

And sky hooked train tracks coloured blue,
For trains that run on rainbows' steam.

Where contrails are used to cut through hue,
And lighten greys in springtimes' dream.

For when days arrive in shades of grey,
It's Beatrix Potter that steals the scene.

LET'S PLAY SPIN

The dark night's gales strayed in with dawn
And while the air was crisp 'twas cold:
They rode life down and iced a frown,
And sun stayed in till noon—all told.
Stolled in and brought along the lunchtime crowds,
All tuckered out from mornings' blight;
No one is made to cheer the cold aloud,
And noon took in a sunny sprite.

Here people come out when sun is high
But lately they feel left high and dry.
Sun stayed awhile and then went in,
Then wind just growled and hissed:

Who knew that noon was sweeping spin?
Not those who feel her dreamy kiss!

REFILL

A sea mist wakes the silent bay.
Its moist grey essence settles down,

To highlight dancers in a spring ballet,
It sent princes and princesses wearing crowns

To shimmy though townlands and gardens, and clay.
And their wands caress dew that sparkles with stars,

That place winters' pardon in an opaque day,
And call out to growth to clear portals to scars.

But day just ignored her and strayed though the chill
She still plays with the idea of a new earth refill.

DA DUM

Day break! and birds were tweeting blows
With wind that settled in nights' soot.
Their songs were piercing ice with prose
That night had packed in metric foot.
Da dum da dum da dum da dum
And there was dawn awake and chilled!

Until two song birds seized the sun:
Each took an end to tug and pull the rain-
Bow blend: And up she flew to run
And flow across the breath of Spain.
Da dum da dum da dum da dum
Now dawn was up and dressed!

Yet people put their jackets on
Though colour seeped through day,
For February's wind just won't move on
Until Lent has had her say.

OUT THERE ON HER OWN

The last few days were braced
For a possibility of rain
To run down springs' affected face.
And clouds were pushed by wind,

Their bellys dipped and curved,
In grey and dark stripped shirts,
With grubby wavy tails reserved,
To dip in sun who dared a random flirt.

March blows up the castles in the air.
Her puff's so large it pumps and pumps,
Until boom! Whoever said
That April was the cruelest month

Only had an eye on voice and tone,
For March is out there on her own.

DOWNPOUR

Here spills are pouring from a sky that's overflowing,
Heavens' tears are falling to the ground,
Hic-cups dropping, plopping, tired, unbeknowing,
If this rain will stop or just keep falling all around.

And the clock ticks down the seconds and the minutes,
Though the drops fog-up its glassy olden face.
And the rain just fell, and man! she drowned the Linnet,
Lashing time with vapours that she found in space.

But when evening came it brought a quiet with it,
And clouds broke to shows of gold and blue:
Where surfers dived and bobbed on seas that blitzed it,
And tomorrow's forecast is for sun to renew.

WHERE TALES ARE FOUND

Sweeping tides make light the sound
By specters made in daytimes' dream.
Now spring is here and scents abound,
Where sun finds love in cloudless schemes.

And sky and sun and air are crowned.
Bewitching day—creating themes
That weeks ago hid all around.
But now non-local love just streams:

For within this springtime—Easter gleams,
And people find their golden seams.

THE SANHEDRIN

Today the air is warm and light.
And birds are tweeting tunes,
To a spring wind that rewrites
The times anointed under spying moon—
Where silver was worth more than life
A Judas walked among his friends.
And plans were made to incite strife
That fear and greed would comprehend.

This costly oily scented swoon
That was redolent of the moon.

IN SPLENDID ISOLATION
(The Last Supper)

A pearly shimmer backlights the play.
A Thursday supper served to light a flame,
Even they who walked the traitors' way were swayed.
They were all friends—even those who were to blame
Were asked to make amends before they, too, were shamed;
Before the heinous deed was pledged to day.

But groups' nature is not contrived above.
But in day-skies that knows a season's weather.
So they sat with sup of wine, food, laughter, love,
And in dimming light they played and prayed together.

Who knew that within hours best friends would deny
An honest truth, and that a good man would die?

GOOD FRIDAY

Who gets to choose the way in which they leave?
Grim reaper stalks in shadow from day one.
But few will walk the path His footsteps cleaved:
This man who lived and died for us, this Son
Of sons; this Friday we take time to grieve,
His essence drifts today to mine deeds done:
Pilate had said the man was free to leave,
His wife had said, 'This is a righteous one.'

A boss was overruled by mobs—deceived,
Another switched on darkness and dimmed the sun.
Today we run again the times when man conceived
To kill and bury the good that makes us one.

This tale is set in books that have had printed runs
From long before we owned our time begun.

HOLY SATURDAY
(*What Empathy Means to Me*)

And now we rest on laurels made from palms.
We surmise about the way He died.
We feel His wounds, and add our own balm.
This man was flogged, tortured, and crucified.
We tell of ways that crowds are now calmed.
They called for blood, but were they satisfied?

We no longer use the rhetoric found in psalms.
We have softer ways to punish and control.
To stop the insurrection in its step.
To mine the minds of our new world souls.

It is the day before the Resurrection.
When dark and light assume their own selection.

Epilogue

OF THE SEA

And as he sang, she sang where day moon
Eavesdropped on a rising sun, and a sea
Swept shushing salmagundi sounds:
Beyond the sands he chanted hope that she'd found
In local lore that she'd outgrown—he's alone,
But near the sea where she lives on her own.

And as he sang, she sang where noontime sun
Burnt sea-grass brown, and unicorn and sea horse
Called around: These were the makers of her
Fiery song, and they danced and spun, as she walked
Along the shore where waves drowned out
The music of her tune and still she sang, until the wind

Reached down and lifted up her words, and the birds
And insects chripped along in time, and his tune
N'er formed to mind or voice, and as it fluttered
Up and up her cry rang out above its sound.
And as she sang, he sang where evening sun
Lit umbra settings formed in auroras' haze,

Then she sighed as horrors lit in holy days,
And through graves where pulpiteers had stood and spun

From tomes the poems and stories long begun
In deathly sermons found in olden ways.
Then she saw her fugue lightly creep in haze—
As beyond the bay a rigadoon arrived to stun,

'Twas here she watched a child at play: Just one.
Until known wailers stole and carved her charm,
And shared it out among themselves—no harm!
And before a one knew to care or hear 'twas done.
And she cried, but they passed her cries around
Between themselves, and it was then she hurt.

And so she learned to croon just to avert.
And she was lost until she found the beauty bound
In words, then she was scared they'd take them back,
So she hid them to be used just for herself,
And she laid them with her life upon a shelf,
And left a half to be shared out by the rest.
And it was into the grinding water,
And the gasping wind's delusion that she bled.

Now she sings where day moon eavesdrops on a
Evening sun, and a sea shushes salmagundi sounds.

The Linnet's Wings Press 2015